A CUT & ASSEMBLE

SHAKER VILLAGE

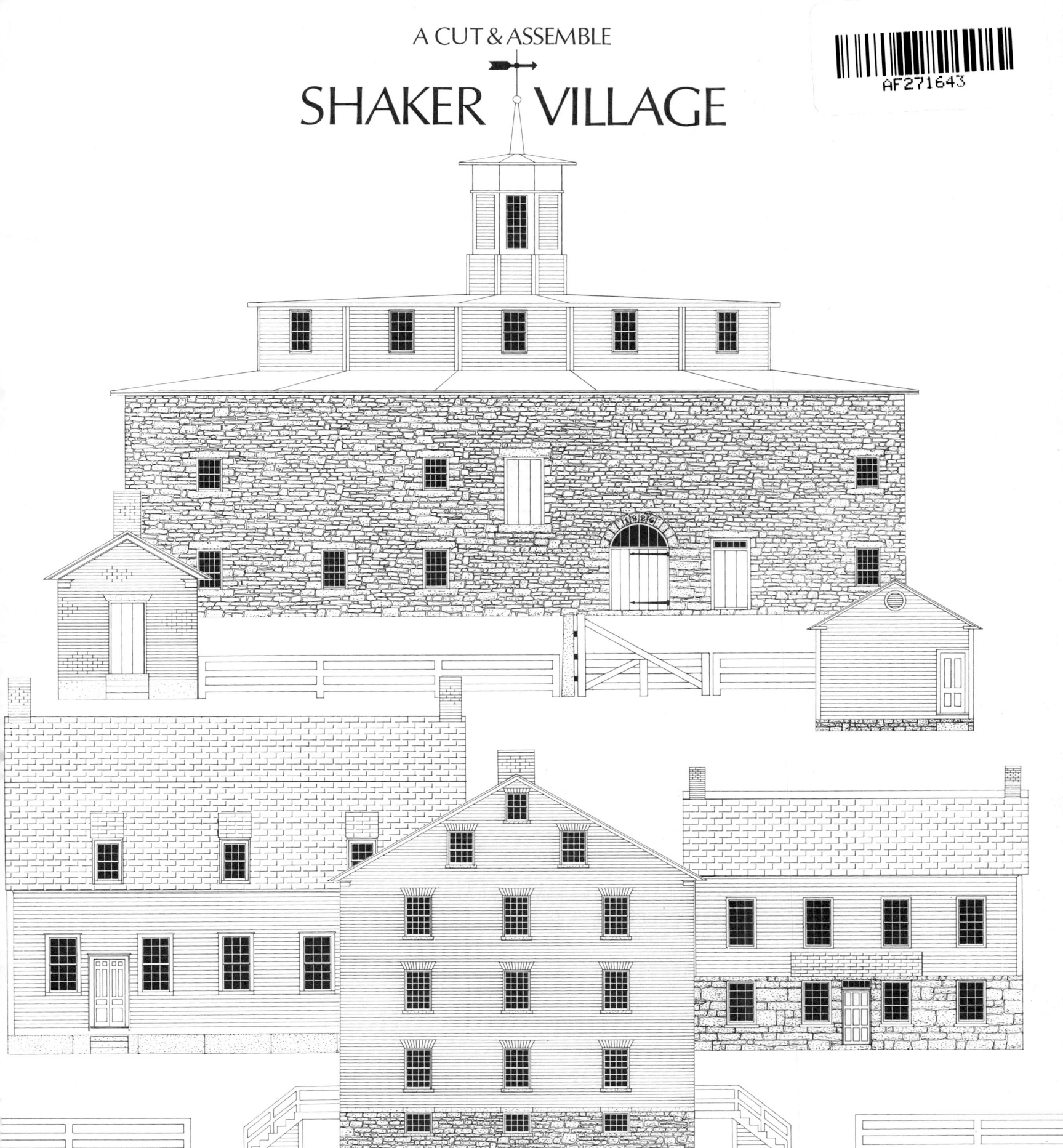

Authentic Architectural Models in H-O Scale

EDMUND V. GILLON JR.

Schiffer Publishing Ltd.

1469 Morstein Road
West Chester, Pennsylvania 19380

Printed in the United States of America.
ISBN: 0-88740-077-9
Published by Schiffer Publishing Ltd.
1469 Morstein Road
West Chester, Pennsylvania 19380

This book may be purchased from the publisher.
Please include $1.50 postage.
Try your bookstore first.

INTRODUCTION

The United Society of Believers in Christ's Second Appearing, as the Shakers officially called themselves, was the most enduring and extensive of all the communal sects established in America. The new nation of the United States offered unlimited opportunities for the establishment of utopian experiments. Political and religious freedom, cheap land, an open society, and quick wealth for the hard-working immigrant were the ingredients required for the perfect society to thrive.

The seed of the Shaker movement was sown in Manchester, England in the late 18th Century. It grew out of a French Protestant sect whose members called themselves "Camisards." Their Manchester counterparts were derisively called "Shakers" on account of their frenzied physical manifestations of religious zeal. A convert to this group, Ann Lee, became its leader in 1770. During a short imprisonment period for Sabbath-breaking, Christ appeared to her and revealed the cause for human depravity to be the sex act. Thereafter, Mother Ann, as she was known, preached her Gospel of sinlessness and celibacy. She was tried by an Anglican church court, found guilty and imprisoned. In a vision, she was directed to go to the American colonies to found the Church of Christ's Second Coming. She left England with eight followers and arrived in New York in 1774.

Two years later, she and her followers joined fellow Shaker John Hocknell, who had purchased several acres of wilderness near Albany. There, the small group labored for several years. In 1781, Mother Ann and her brother, William Lee, undertook a two-year missionary journey into Massachusetts and Connecticut. There, they were subjected to physical abuse by unruly mobs. In 1783, Mother Ann and her brother returned to New York State, and a year later, they both died.

Strong new leaders appeared to continue her work and soon, Shaker communities were established in New York State, Massachusetts, Connecticut, New Hampshire, Maine, Ohio and Kentucky. These villages flourished and converts to Shakerism numbered in the thousands. Economic growth was exceptional. Communism provided the inspiration for the dedication to group welfare and provided the discipline needed to maintain the maximum production of goods. Agriculture was the primary means of support for the communities, but consumer goods were also produced and found an eager market in the outside, non-Shaker world. Packaged seeds (the first to be produced in America), flat brooms (a Shaker innovation), chairs, cloaks, and round boxes, were popular items produced by the industrial Shakers.

The Shakers saw no virtue in hard labor when it could be relieved by machines. The following is a list of the devices invented by Shakers to eliminate unnecessary labor: the clothespin, the cut nail and the circular saw (invented by a Harvard sister), the screw propeller, planing and fertilizing machines, a silk reeling machine, an apple corer, and a pea sheller.

The Shaker communities reached their zenith of wealth, membership and achievement at the end of the Civil War. Many factors led to their decline including loss of their property in Kentucky, the inability to compete with late 19th-Century industrialism, the departure of young members of the group, the decline in leadership qualities, and the advancing age of most of their members. The 20th Century saw the closing of the majority of the communities. Only two orders remain, one at Sabbath Lake, Maine, and the other at Canterbury, New Hampshire. Today, membership numbers less than half a dozen.

The Shaker village at Hancock, Massachusetts, has been established as a museum, and a visit there leaves one with a vivid sense of the Shaker legacy that once enriched our national culture.

THE FOLLOWING IS A LIST OF SHAKER COMMUNITIES OPEN TO THE PUBLIC

HANCOCK, MASSACHUSETTS 1790
SABBATHDAY LAKE, MAINE (Poland Spring) 1793
CANTERBURY, NEW HAMPSHIRE 1793
PLEASANT HILL, KENTUCKY 1814

SHAKER MUSEUMS

"FRUITLANDS", HARVARD, MASSACHUSETTS
SHAKER HISTORICAL MUSEUM, SHAKER HEIGHTS, OHIO
SHAKER MUSEUM, OLD CHATHAM, NEW YORK

BIBLIOGRAPHY

Andrews, Edward Deming. *The People Called Shakers*. Oxford University Press.
_____ , *Shaker Furniture*. Dover Publications.
Lassiter, William Lawrence. *Shaker Architecture*. Vantage Press.
Miller, Amy Bess. *Hancock Shaker Village/The City of Peace*. Hancock Shaker Village.
Pierson, Elmer and Neal, Julia. *The Shaker Image*. New York Graphic Society.
Rose, Milton C. and Emily Mason. *Shaker Tradition and Design*. Bonanza Books.
Schiffer, Herbert. *Shaker Architecture*. Schiffer Publishing Ltd.

INSTRUCTIONS

The following basic tools are recommended: an x-acto knife & #11 blade; a scoring tool to create folds; a burnishing tool for pressing down glue tabs in areas difficult to reach with fingertips; a clear plastic triangle to use as a cutting and scoring guide; and Elmers glue. Dots indicate glue tabs, arrows indicate scores, (R.S. and arrows indicate reverse scores) to reverse score make pinpoints near ends of score line, turn piece over and score between pinpoints, x's indicate areas to be cut out. Apply glue to tabs only, not to the receiving surface. Do not apply too much glue—it will seep out and mar the printed surface.

Circles indicate eaves. To create the overhang, cut underneath base of gable triangle to corner fold line.

Doors may be opened by cutting top, right and bottom edges, then score left edge and bend in or out as desired.

DWELLING

The austere three-and-a-half story brick dwelling house was built in 1828, at the Shaker village of Watervliet, New York. The basement contains the kitchen, baking room, dining room and pantries.

The three main floors consist of identical bedrooms.

Surmounting the slate roof is a bell tower which summoned sect members at rising time (4:30 a.m. in summer and autumn, and 5:30 a.m. during the cold winter months) and announced the three meals of the day.

The dwelling house bears a strong resemblance to the early New England textile mills of the same period. The foundation is built of irregular slabs of fieldstone, and the window sills are of limestone.

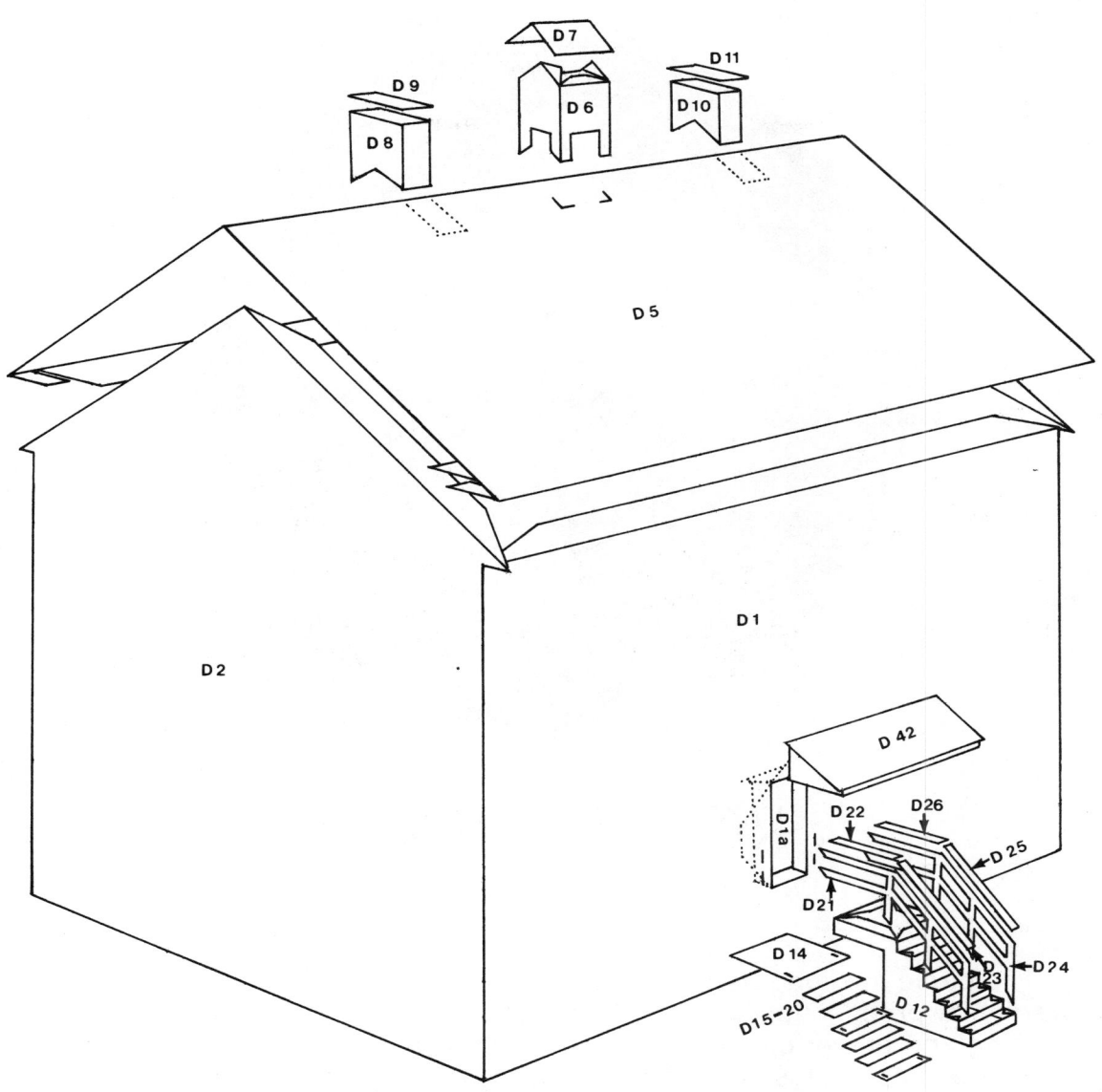

ROUND BARN

The circle has long been regarded as a perfect form. That the Shakers had a particular predilection for such a perfect form is shown in their sewing circles, singing and prayer circles. Also consider the popular Shaker artifacts such as their round hats, rugs, boxes and the round drawer pulls and hand-rests of their chaste furniture. It is not surprising then that they chose the circle as a plan arrangement for the great stone barn erected in Hancock, Massachusetts, in 1826. It served as a model for the many circular barns built along the Western frontier in the last two decades of the 19th Century.

The Hancock barn is an enormous structure measuring 270 feet in circumference. The stone walls are 21-feet high and are between two and a half and three and a half feet thick. The second-story balcony that encircles the interior open space is entered by a ramp and a great door through which a hay wagon may drive in a circle unloading its hay into the mow. The heads of the cattle which were kept in stalls under the wagon drive faced into the mow from which they were fed. In the middle of the mow an octagon of posts support the cupola and form a base from which the rafters radiate. Four great windmill-like braces span the mow from octagon to posts on the drive floor. The cupola pierces the center of the roof's 14-sided windowed monitor. The sides of the octagonal cupola alternate between windows for light and louvered openings that lessen the danger of spontaneous combustion.

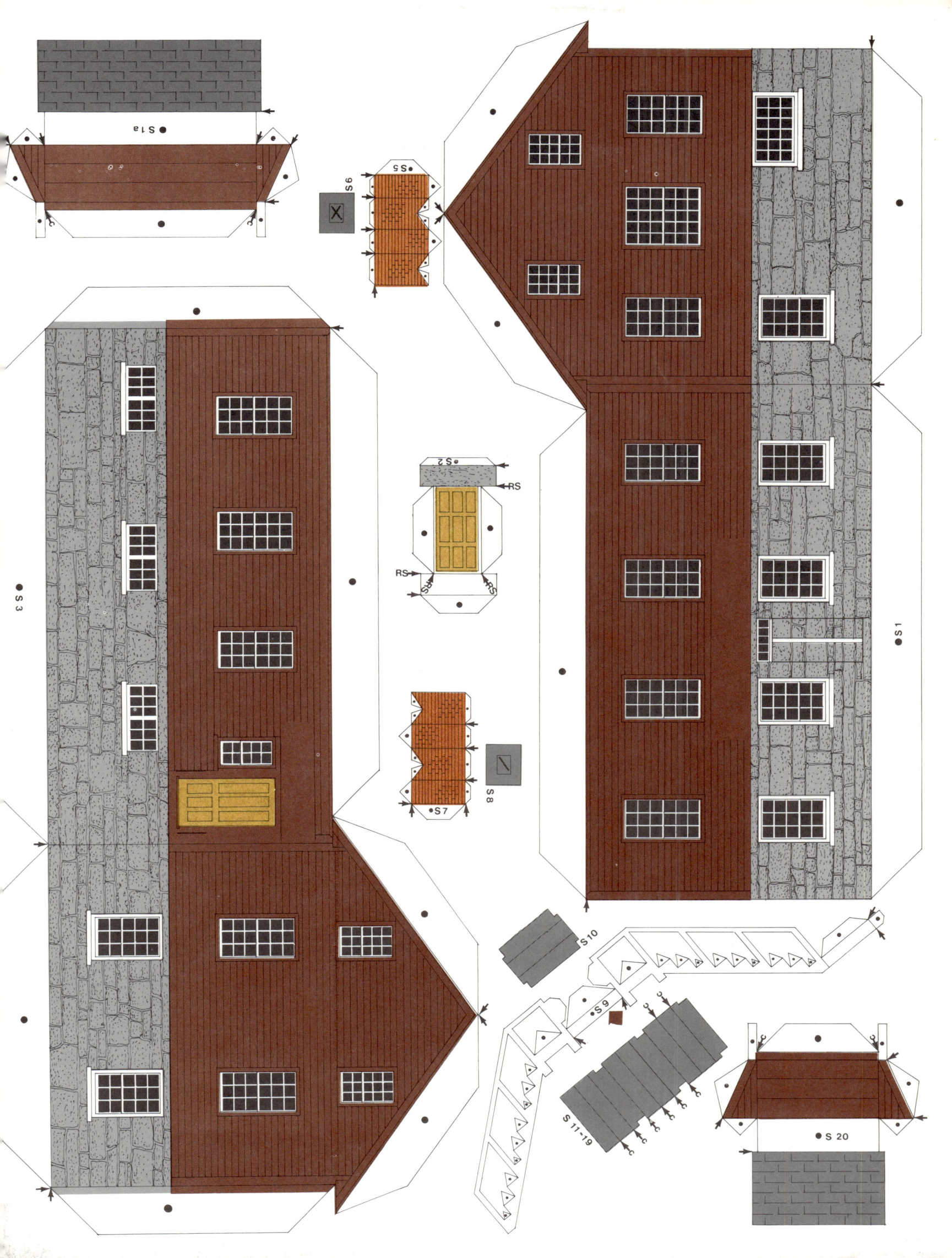

S 1a

S 6

S 5

X

S 3

S 2

RS

RS RS RS

S 7

S 8

S 1

S 10

S 9

S 11-19

S 20

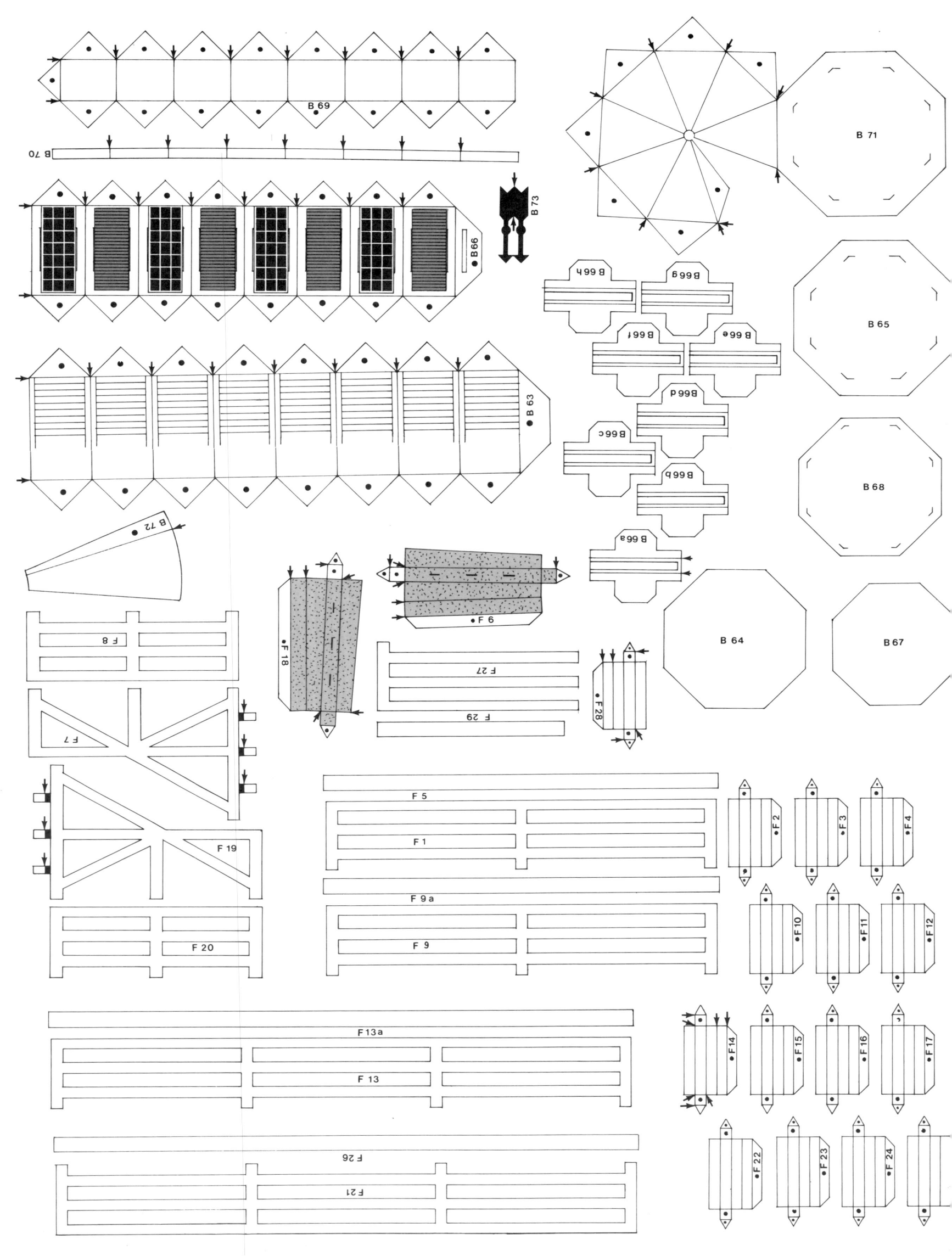

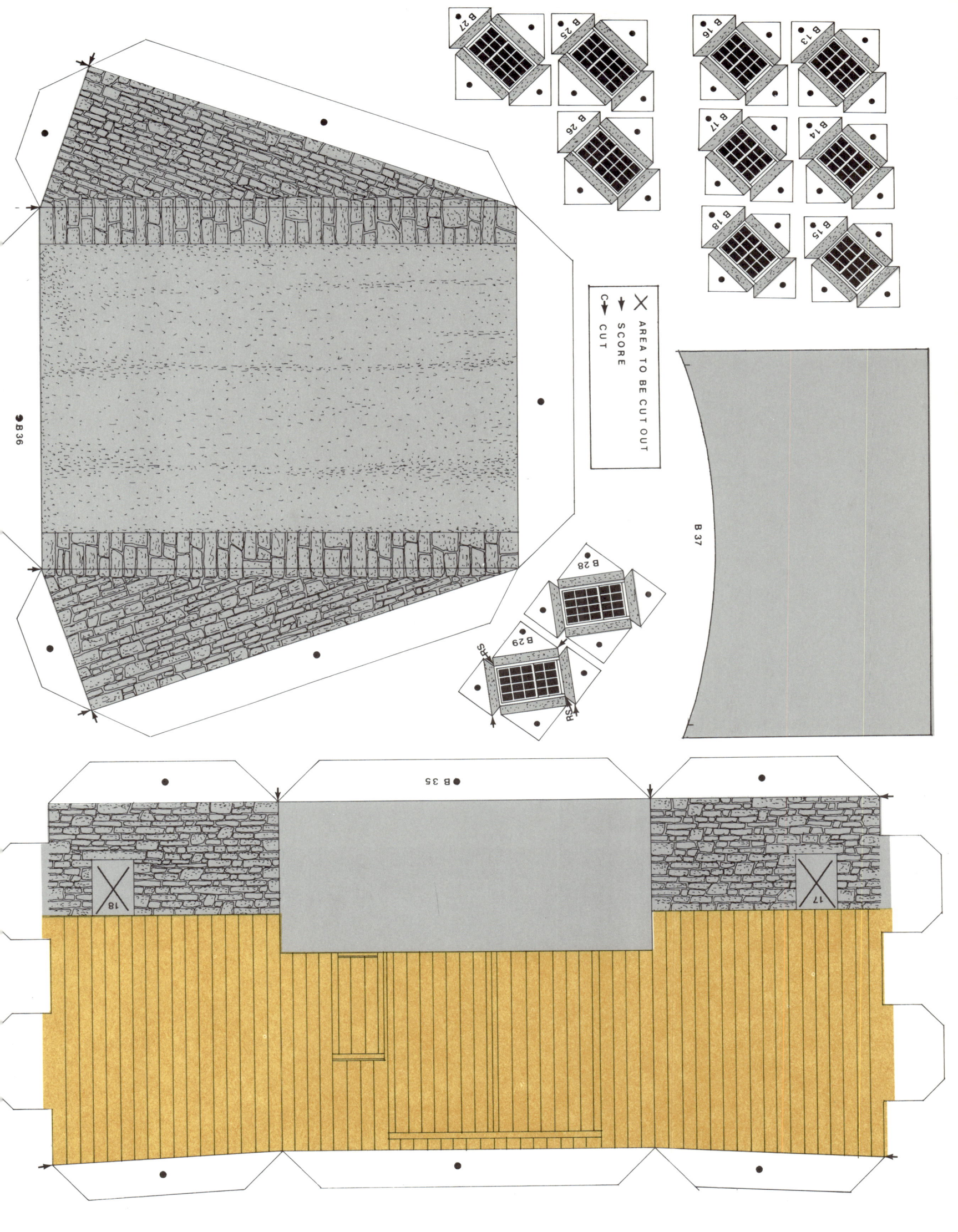

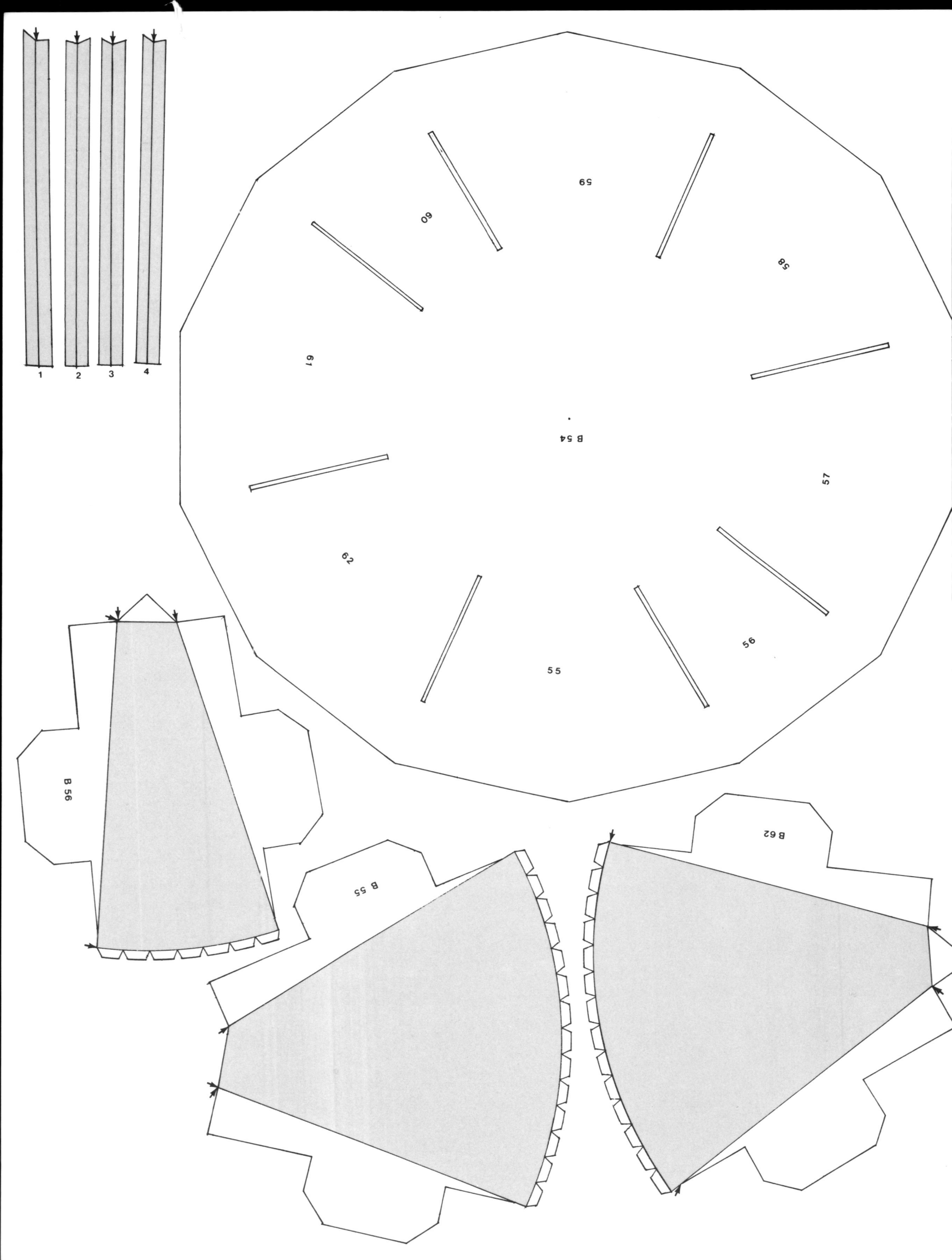

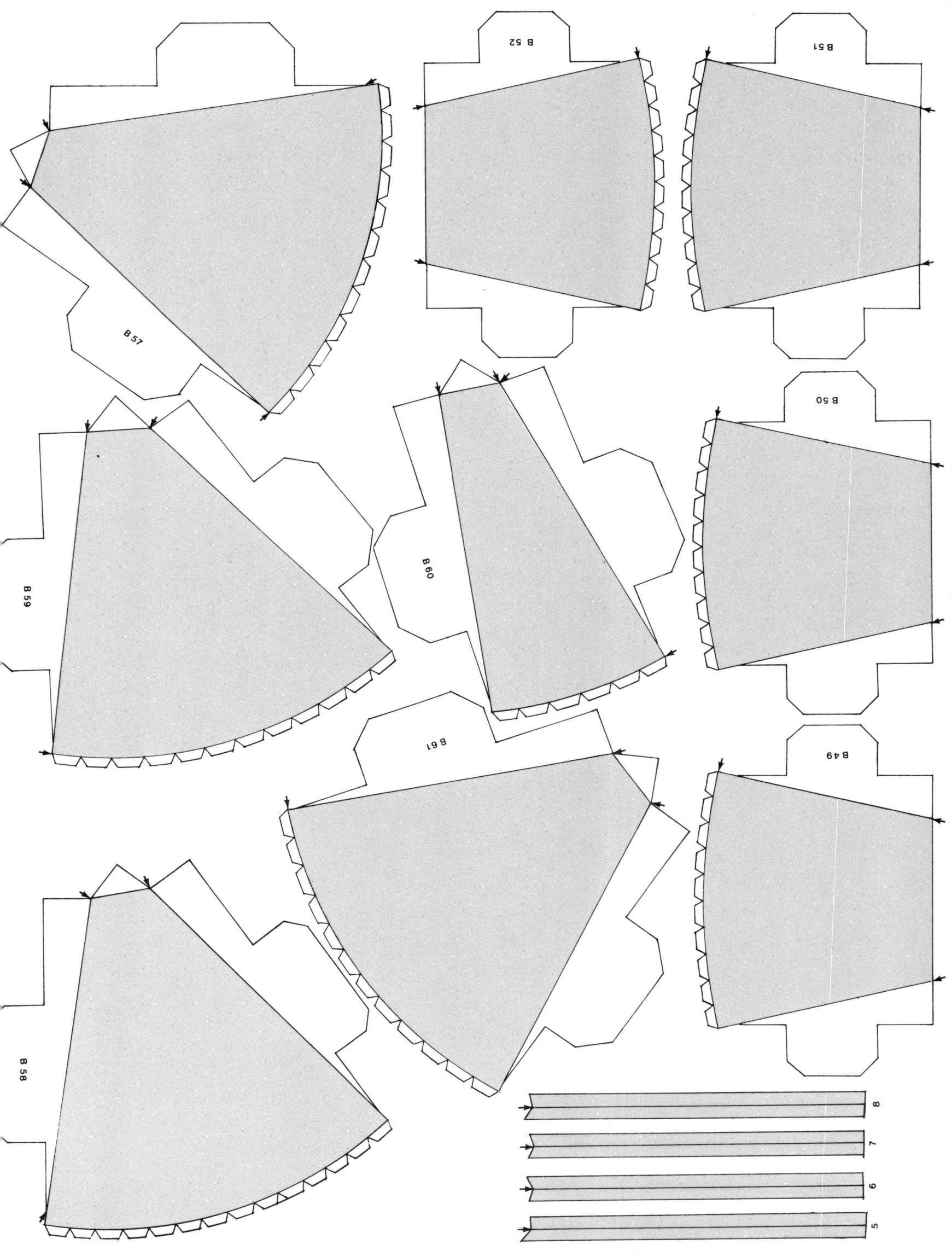

B 52

B 51

B 57

B 50

B 59

B 60

B 49

B 61

B 58

8

7

6

5

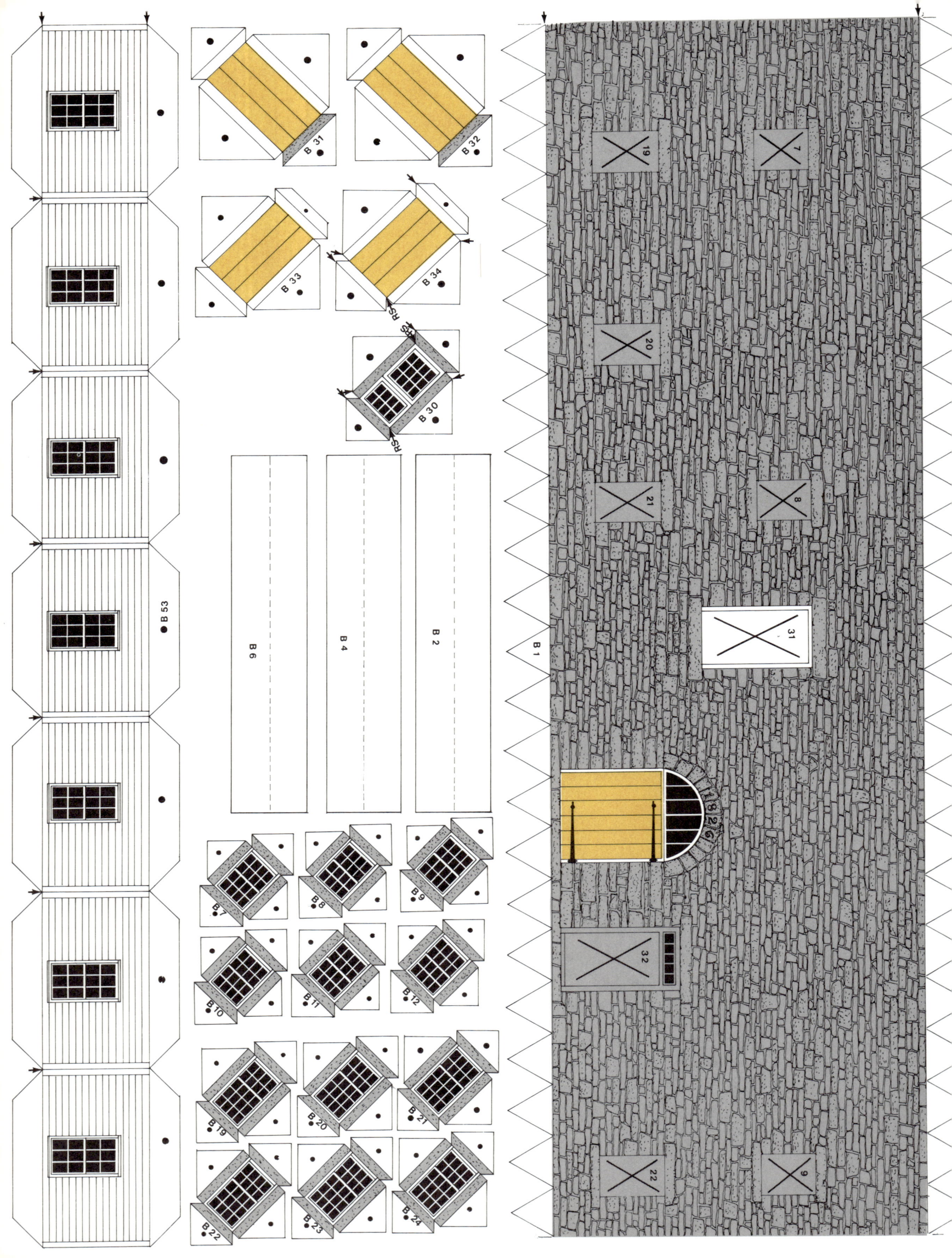

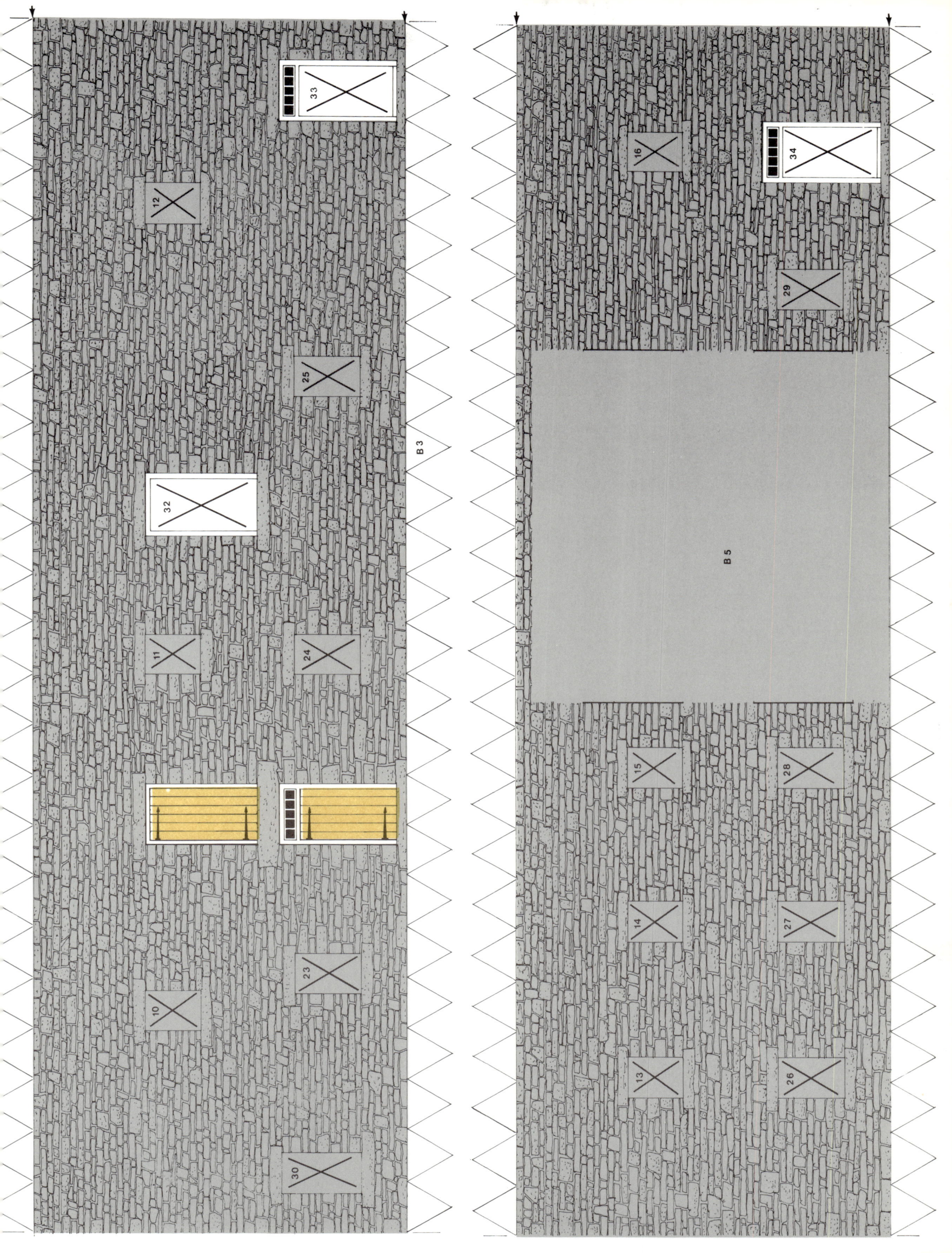

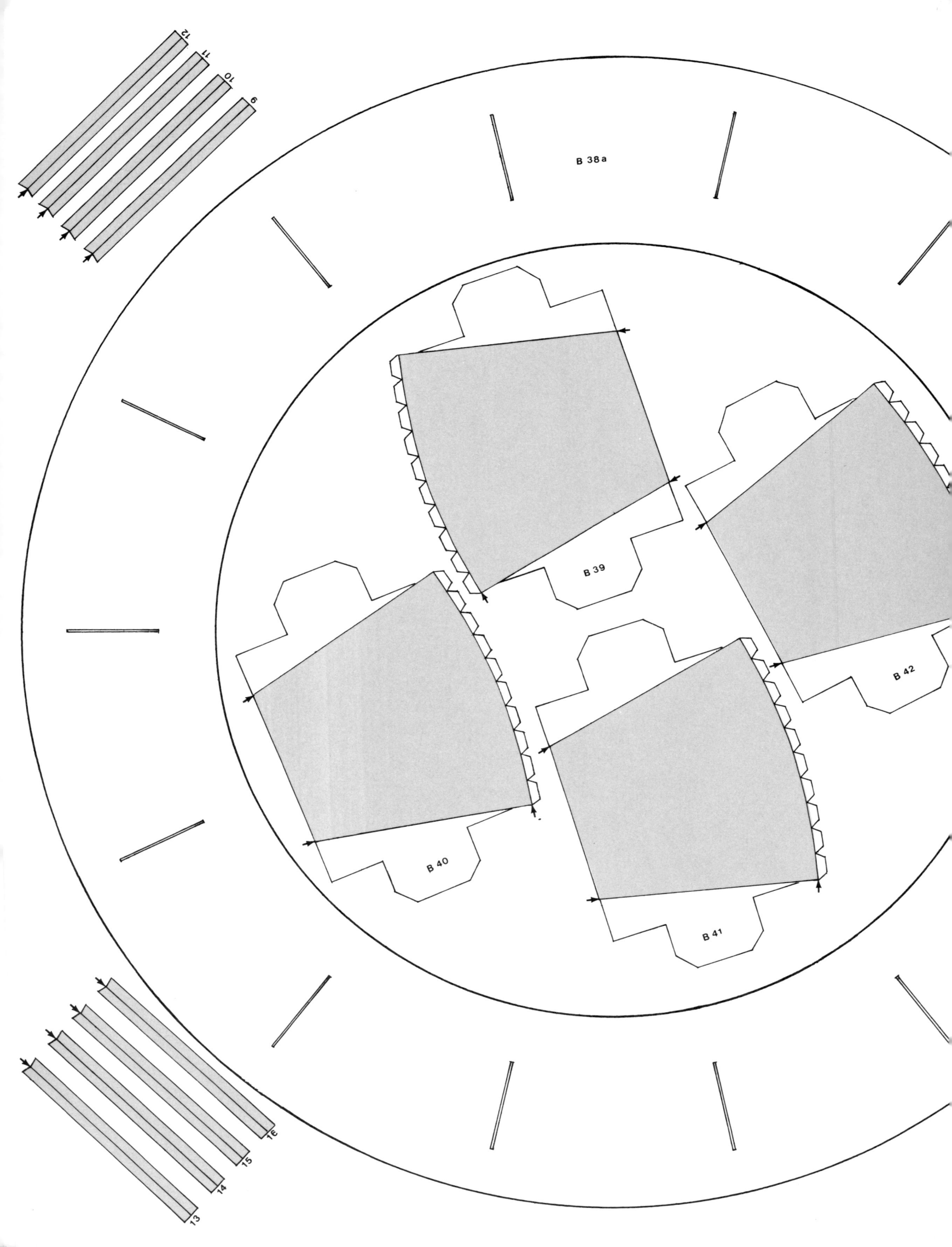

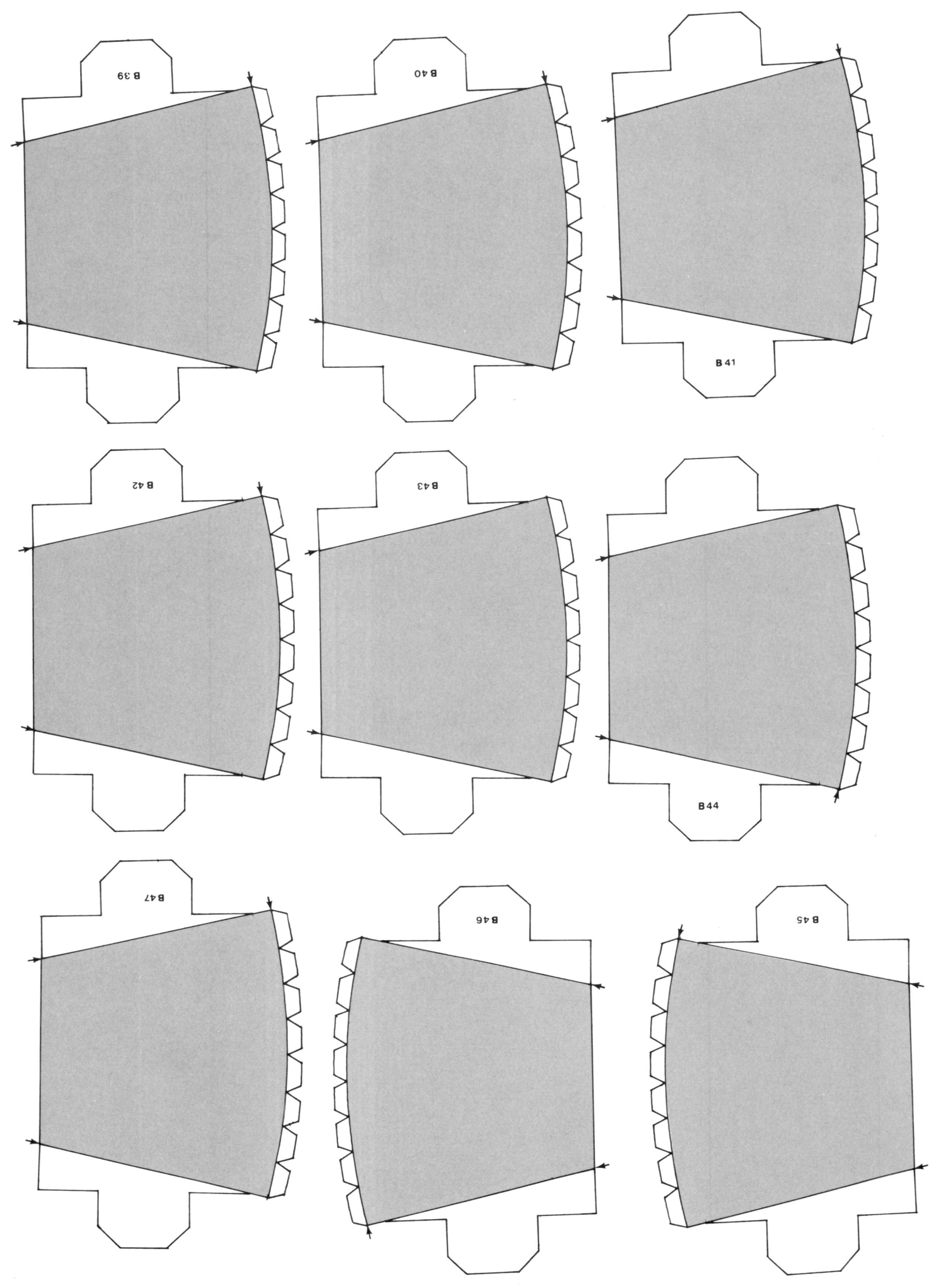

B 39

B 40

B 41

B 42

B 43

B 44

B 47

B 46

B 45

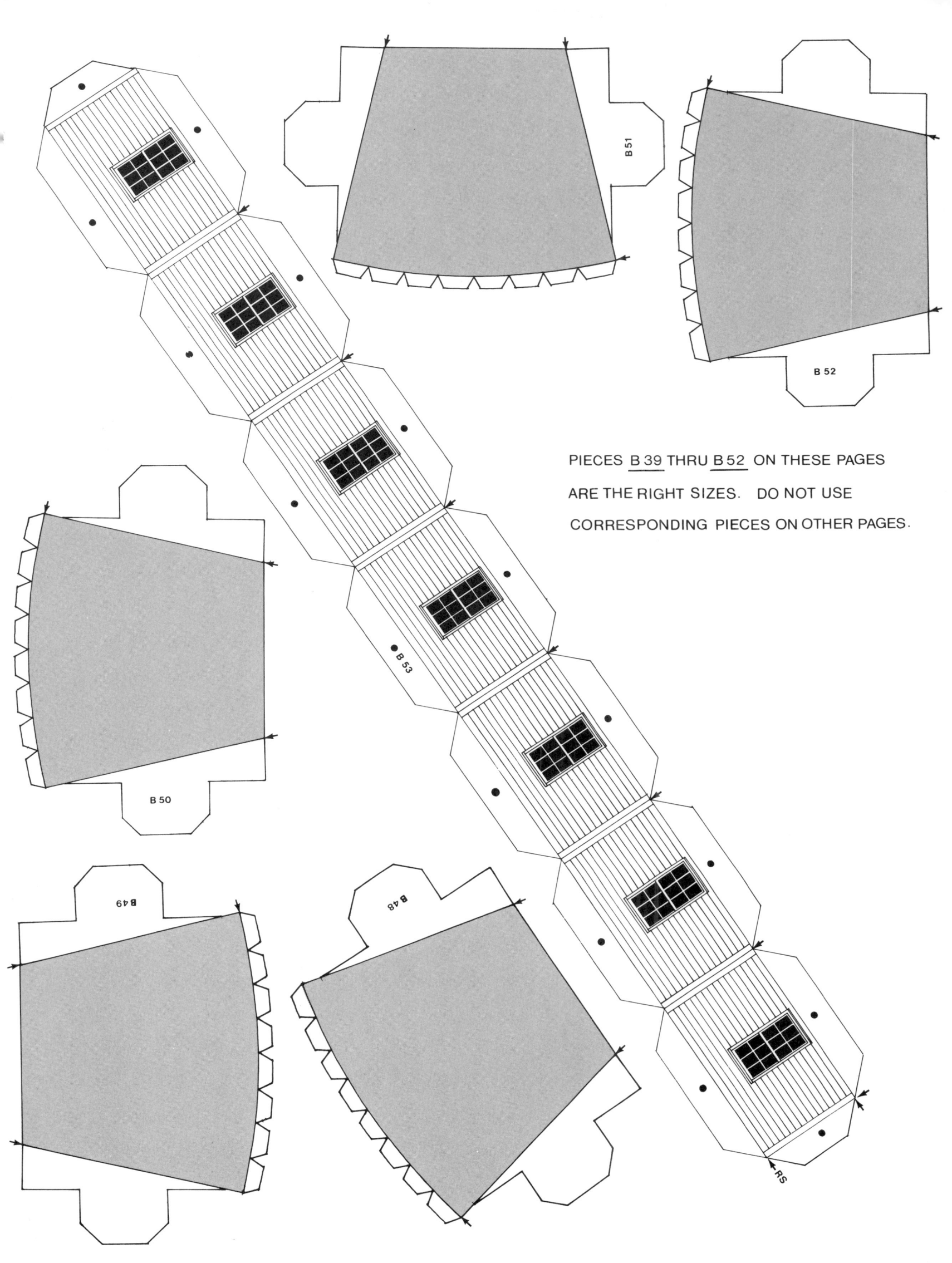

B 51

B 52

B 50

B 53

B 49

B 48

RS

PIECES B 39 THRU B 52 ON THESE PAGES
ARE THE RIGHT SIZES. DO NOT USE
CORRESPONDING PIECES ON OTHER PAGES.

B 43

B 44

B 45

B 46

B 47

B 48

B
a b c d

e f g
B

22
21
20
19
18
17

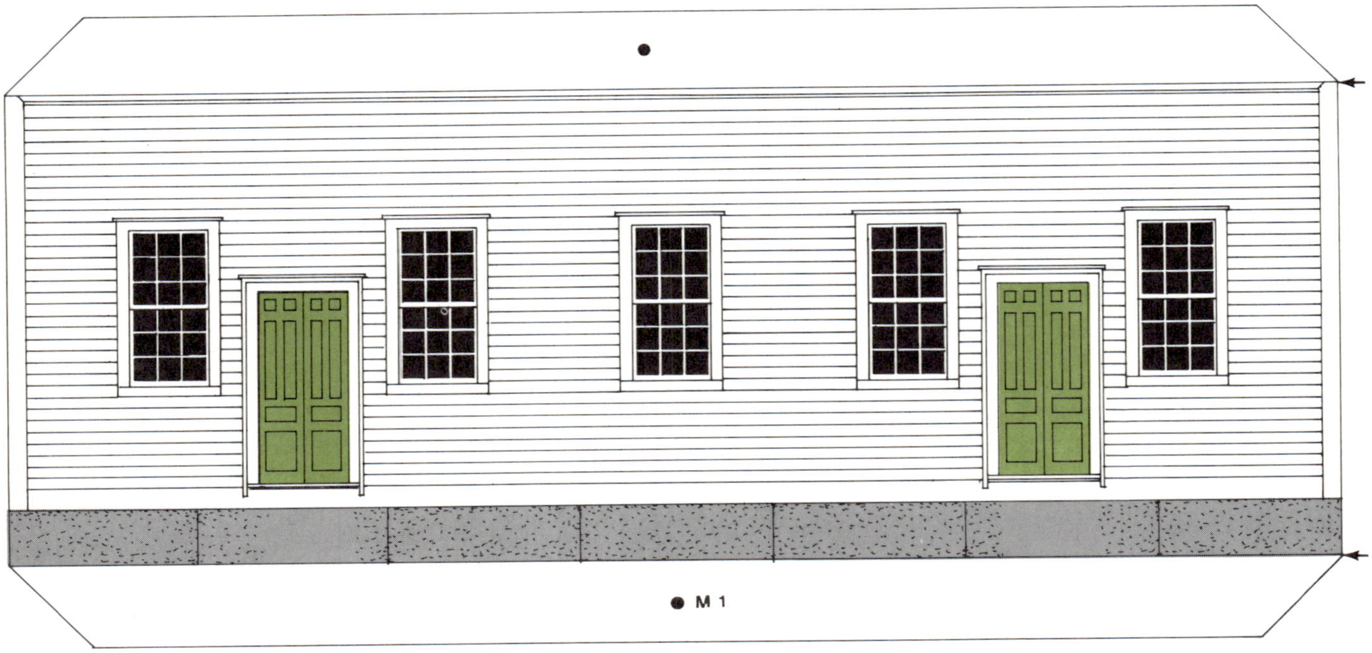

M 1

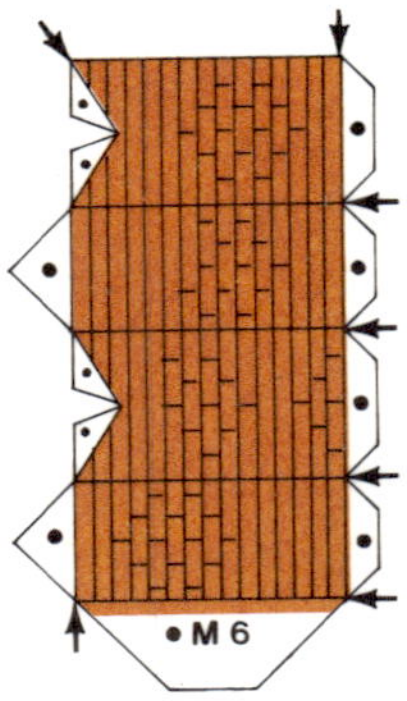

M 6

M 7

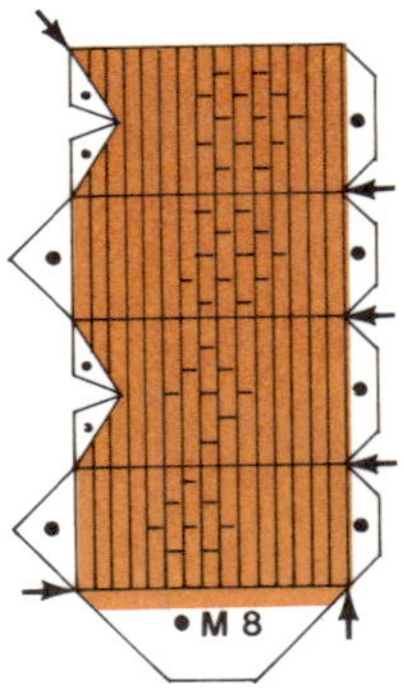

M 8

M 9

M 5

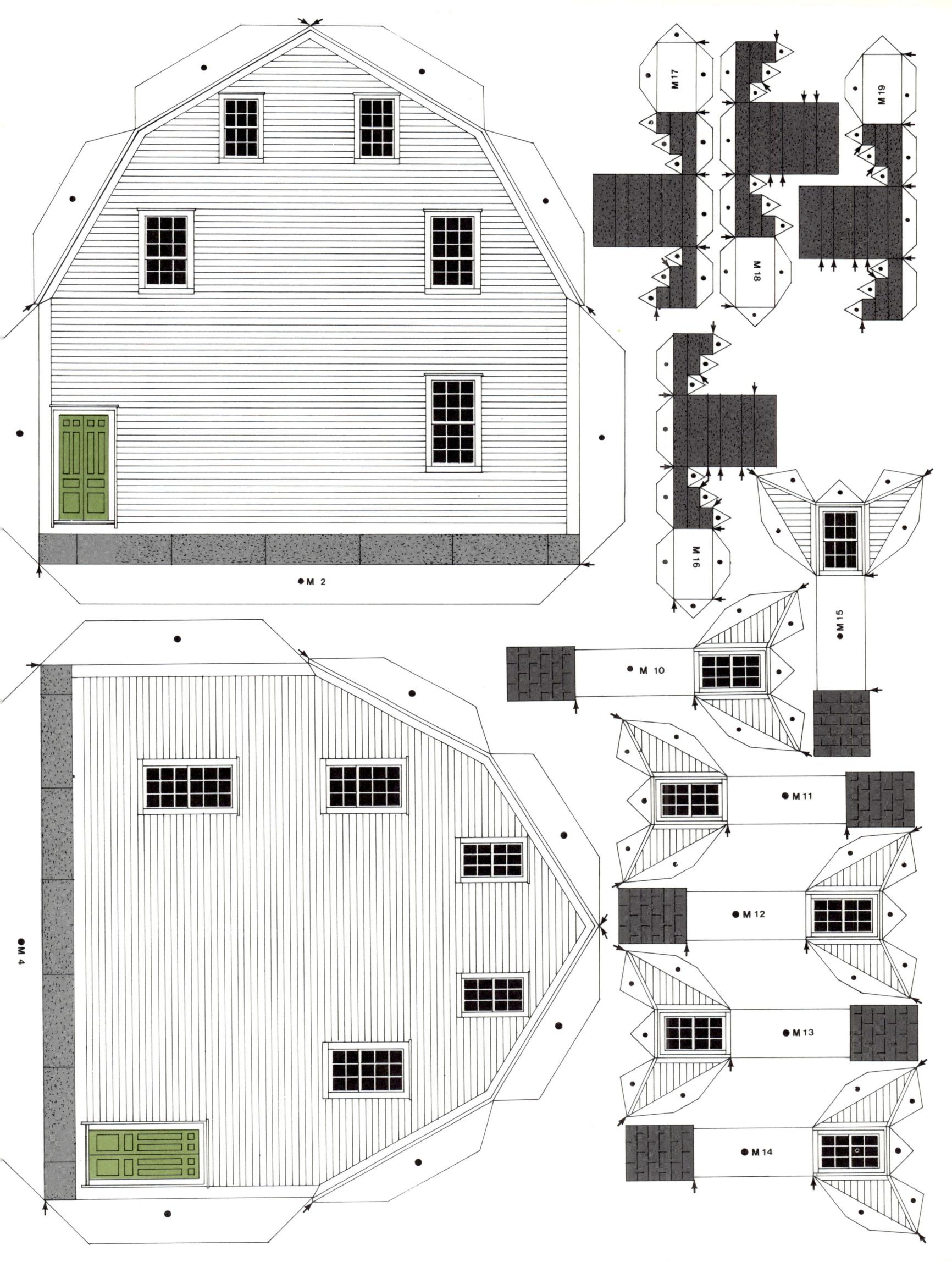

M 2

M 4

M 10

M 11

M 12

M 13

M 14

M 15

M 16

M 17

M 18

M 19

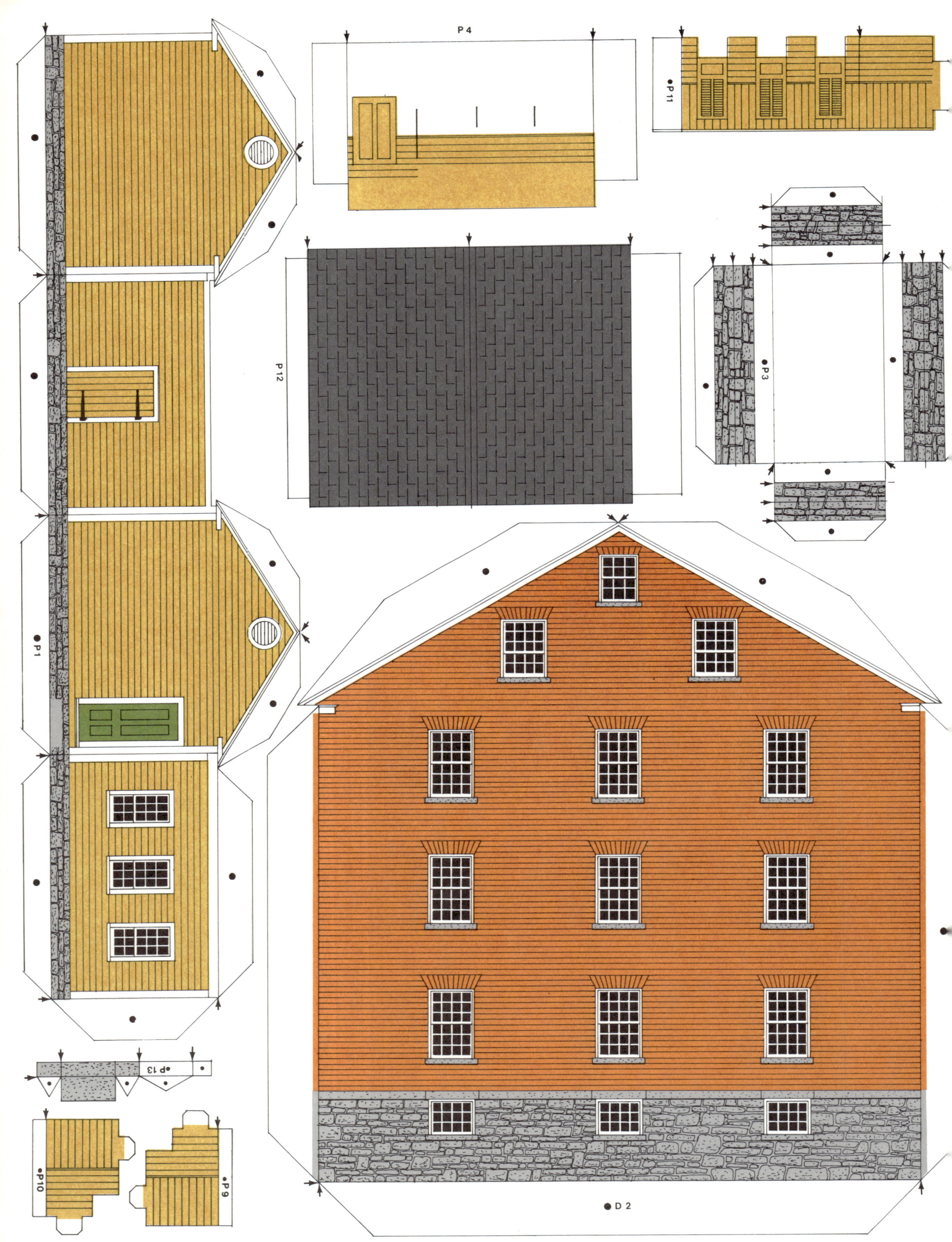

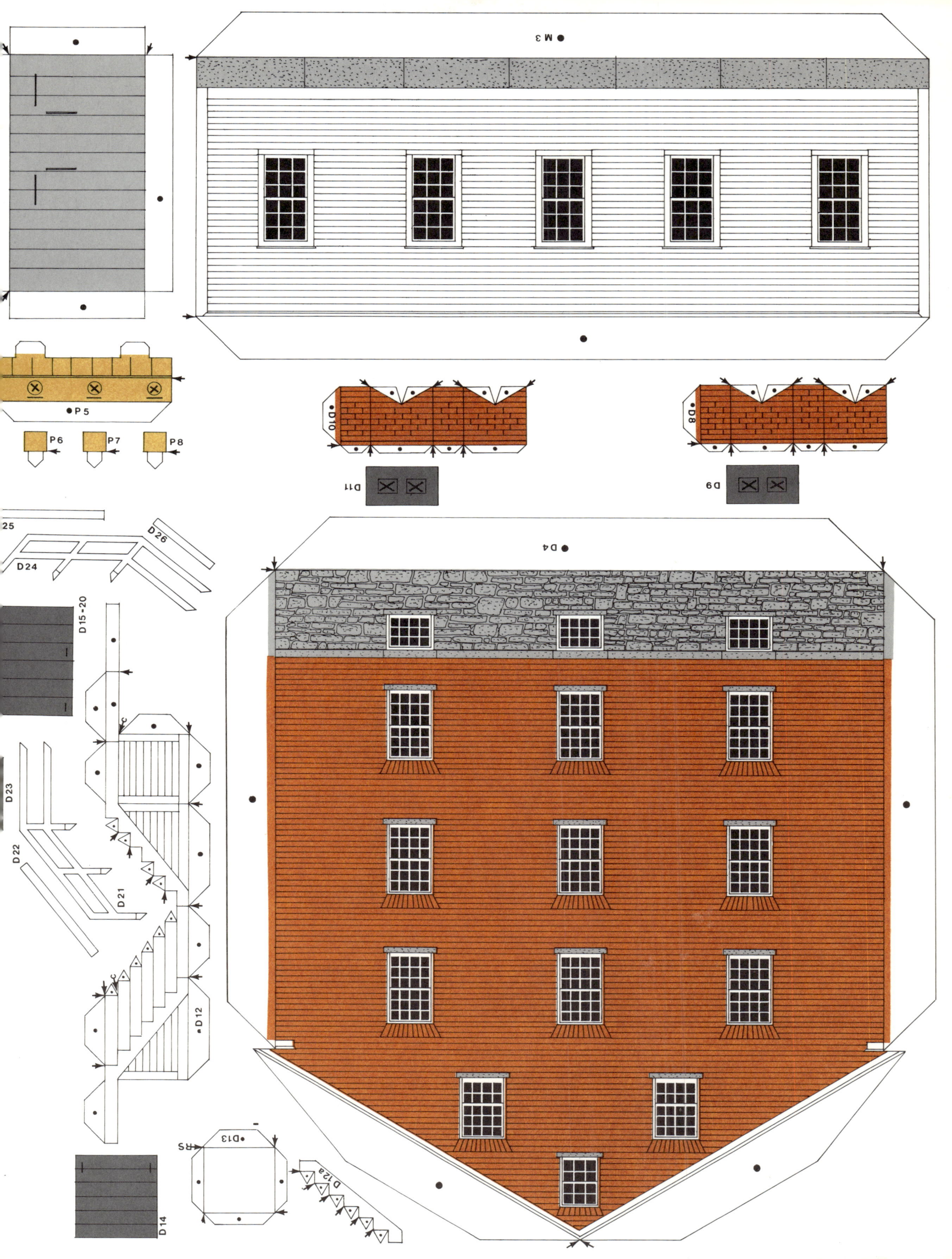

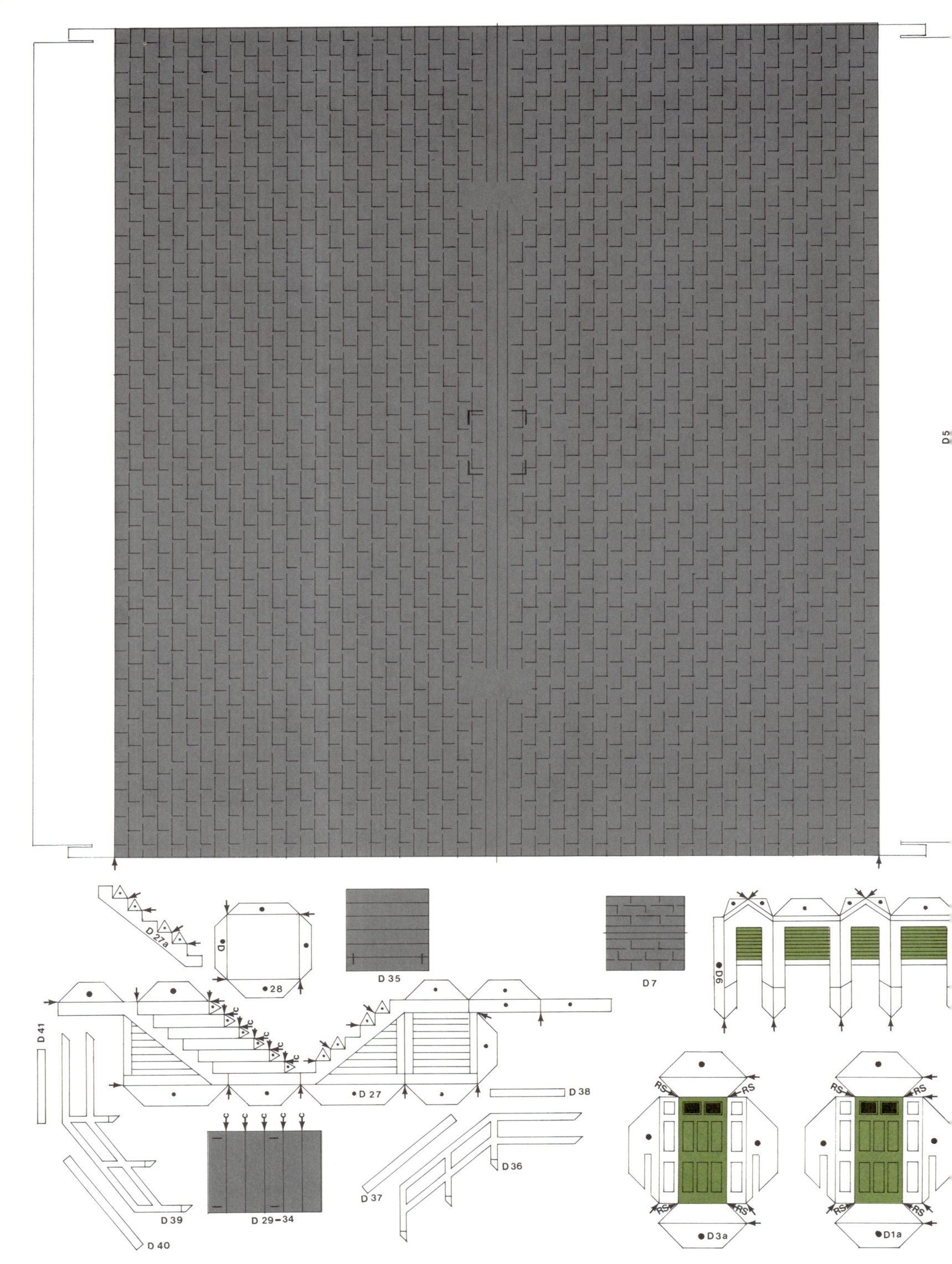

D 5

D 27a

D

28

D 35

D 7

D 6

D 41

D 27

D 38

D 36

D 37

D 39

D 29—34

D 40

D 3a

D1a

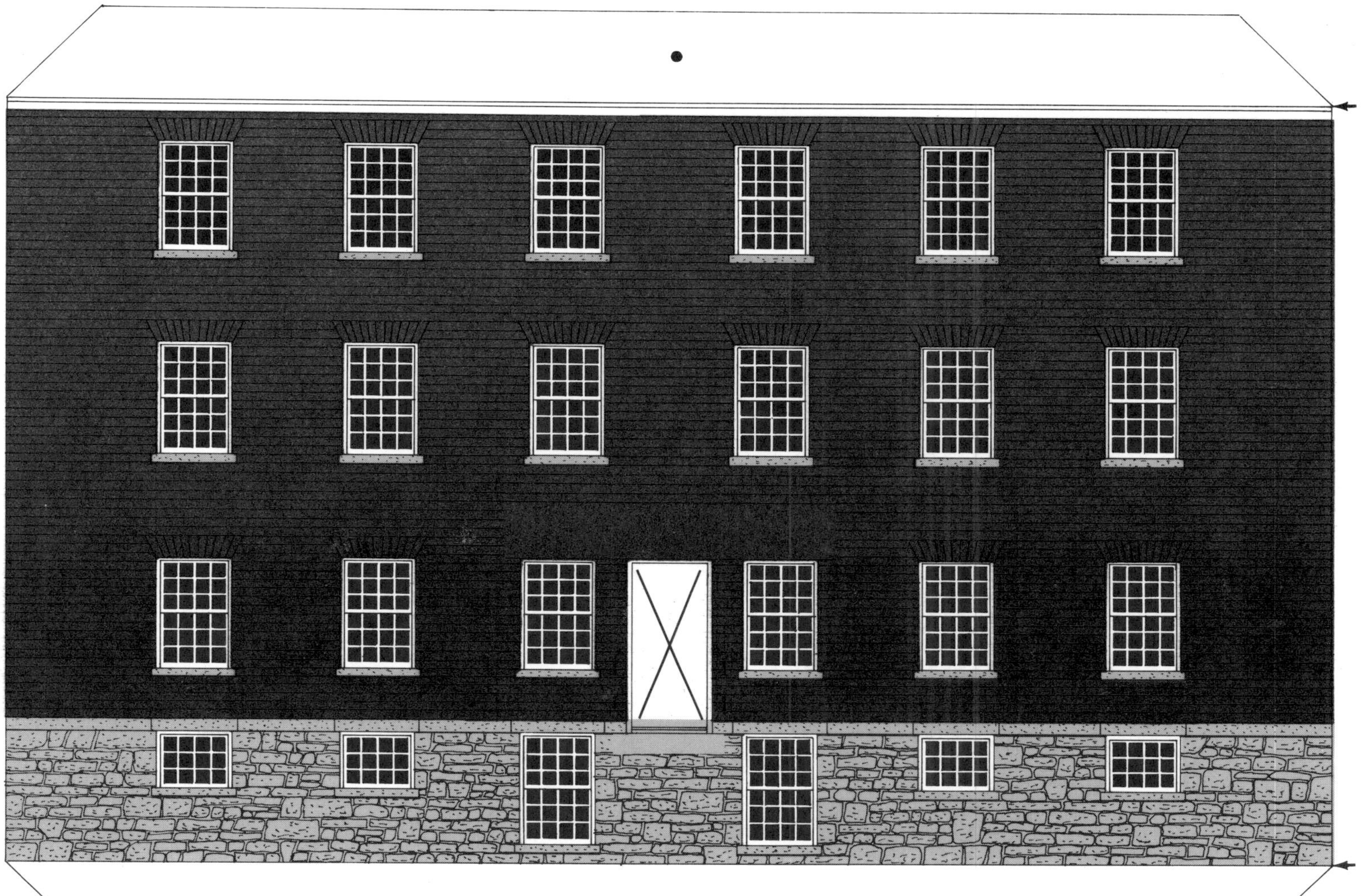

● D1

● D3

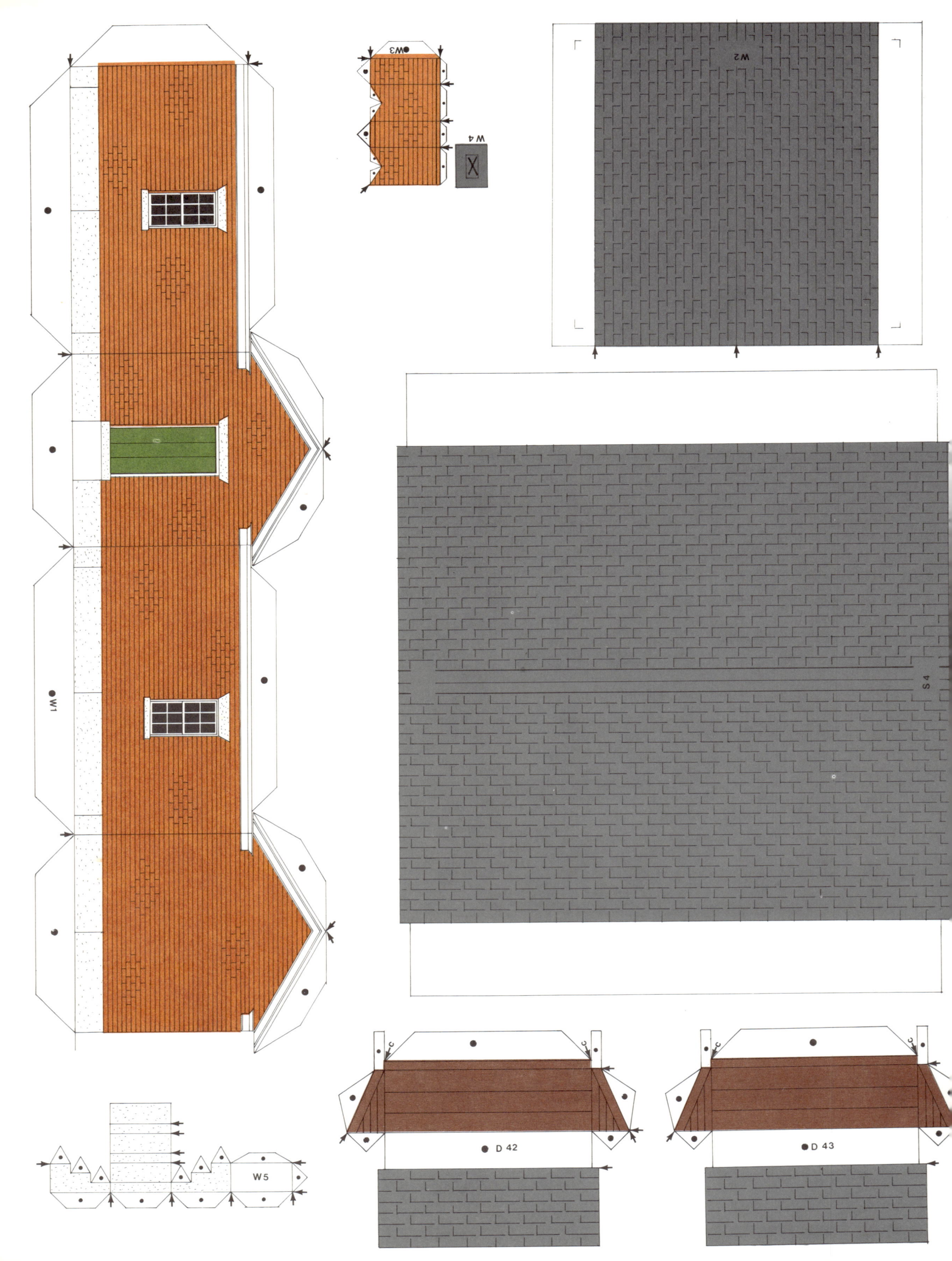

W3

W4

W2

W1

S4

W5

D 42

D 43

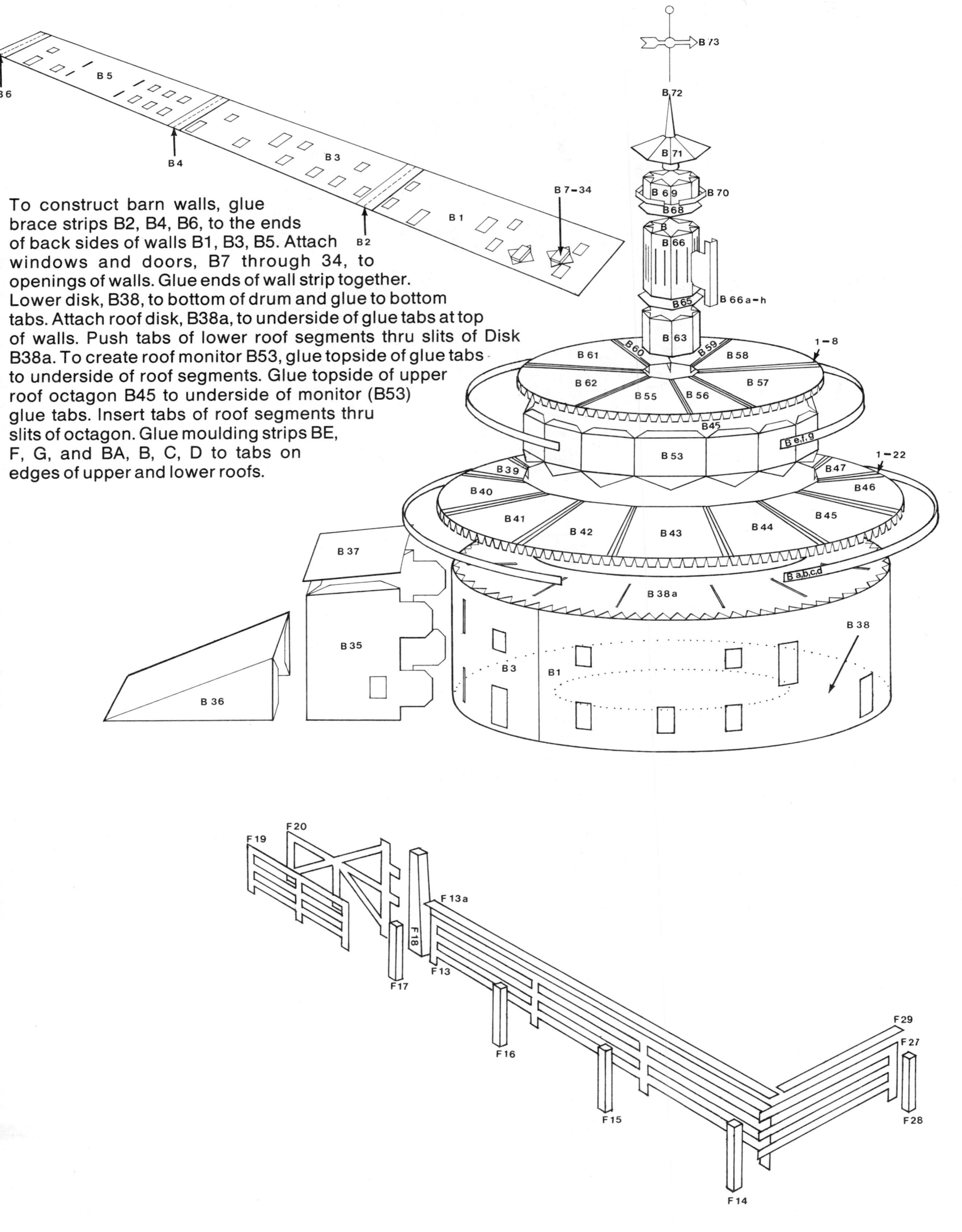

To construct barn walls, glue brace strips B2, B4, B6, to the ends of back sides of walls B1, B3, B5. Attach windows and doors, B7 through 34, to openings of walls. Glue ends of wall strip together. Lower disk, B38, to bottom of drum and glue to bottom tabs. Attach roof disk, B38a, to underside of glue tabs at top of walls. Push tabs of lower roof segments thru slits of Disk B38a. To create roof monitor B53, glue topside of glue tabs to underside of roof segments. Glue topside of upper roof octagon B45 to underside of monitor (B53) glue tabs. Insert tabs of roof segments thru slits of octagon. Glue moulding strips BE, F, G, and BA, B, C, D to tabs on edges of upper and lower roofs.

MEETINGHOUSE

The gambrel-roofed meetinghouse was moved to Hancock, Massachusetts in 1962, from its original site in Shirley in the central part of the State. It replaces an identical building on the site that had been built in 1785. Moses Johnson, of Enfield, New Hampshire, constructed both buildings. Johnson, a Shaker, built seven similar meetinghouses in other Shaker communities.

The two-and-a-half-story structure closely resembles the ubiquitous gambrel-roofed cottages of the period that were scattered throughout New England and in the Hudson River valley. The ground floor consisted of one unobstructed space with benches along the walls. The openess was necessary for the ritualistic dancers that were part of the Shaker service. The room was entered through two separate doors on the front side of the building. One door was for the brethren, the other for the sisters. The doors on the ends of the room were reserved for the male and female clergy. The second floor consisted of two sets of rooms, used by the elders and eldresses as living quarters and offices. The millennial laws recorded at New Lebanon in 1821 dictated that white paint and gambrel-roofs be allowed for meetinghouses only.

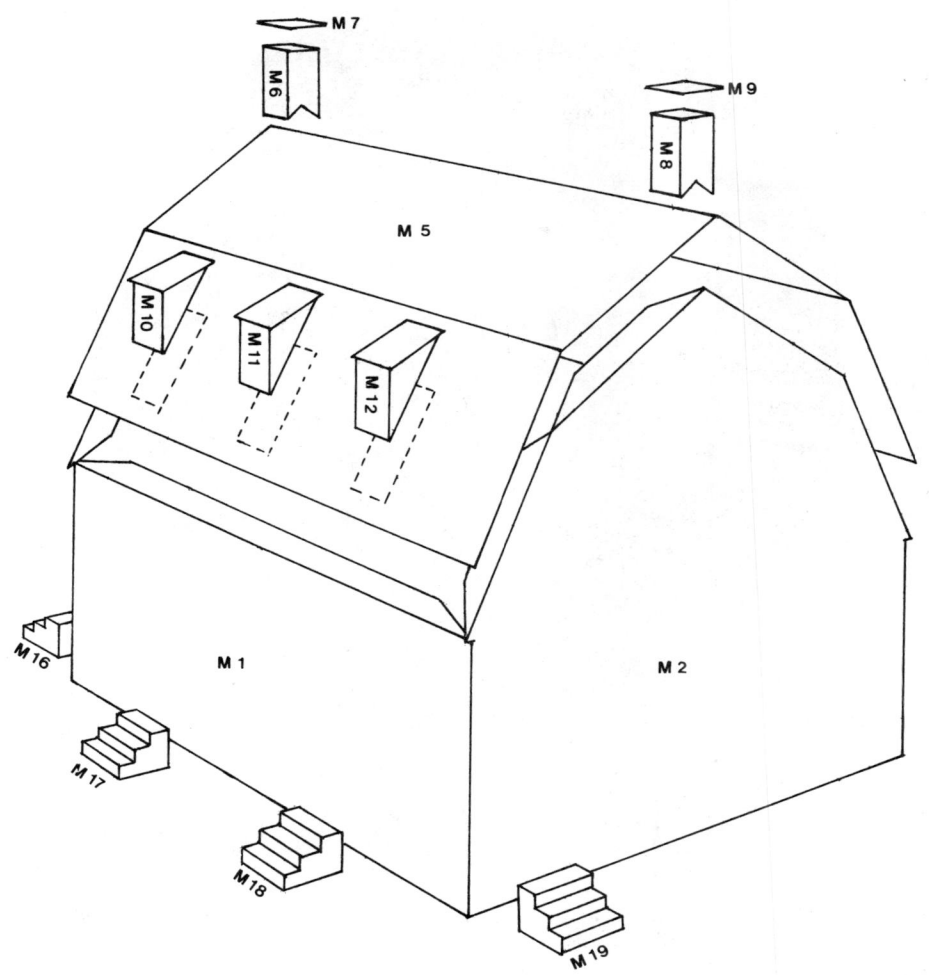

SCHOOLHOUSE

Mother Ann, the Shaker's founder stressed the importance of education. The education of children under the care of the Shakers was conceded to be superior to that in other rural communities. Each shaker village had its own school house and in districts where no other school existed, non-Shakers were admitted. Emphasis was placed on a practical and strong moral education and careful training by example and admonition. An older sister served as school mistress. The boys attended school in winter; the girls attended summer school with time off to help with kitchen chores during the canning season.

The school house was built in 1839 in Mount Lebanon, New York. The first building is constructed of irregular limestone blocks. The building has upper and lower classrooms. The front door had an overhanging canopy. This is duplicated over the rear door which is the entrance to the second-floor classroom. A small kitchen occupies space along the gabled end wall of the lower classroom.

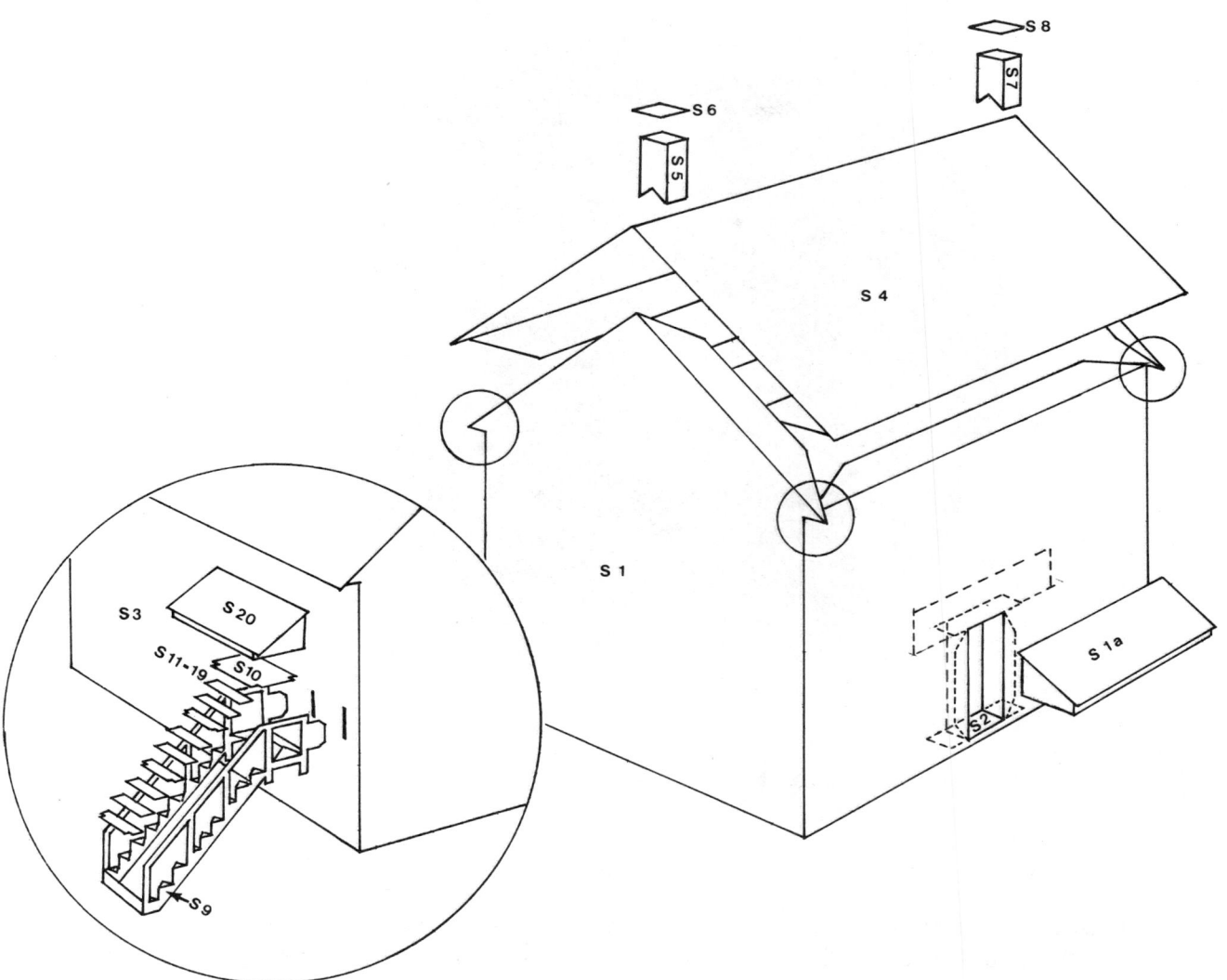

S 8

S 7

S 6

S 5

S 4

S 1

S 3

S 20

S 11-19

S 10

S 9

S 2

S 1a

PRIVY

This small frame building is a three-seater facility, containing individual booths entered through louvered half doors. The toilet area occupies approximately half the floor space and is entered through a door at the right corner of the gabled front. The remaining space consists of a sunken manure pit with a door on the exterior wall for removal of accumulated material. Three windows provide ample ventilation in the toilet area. Round louvered openings in the gables provide cross ventilation in the attic.

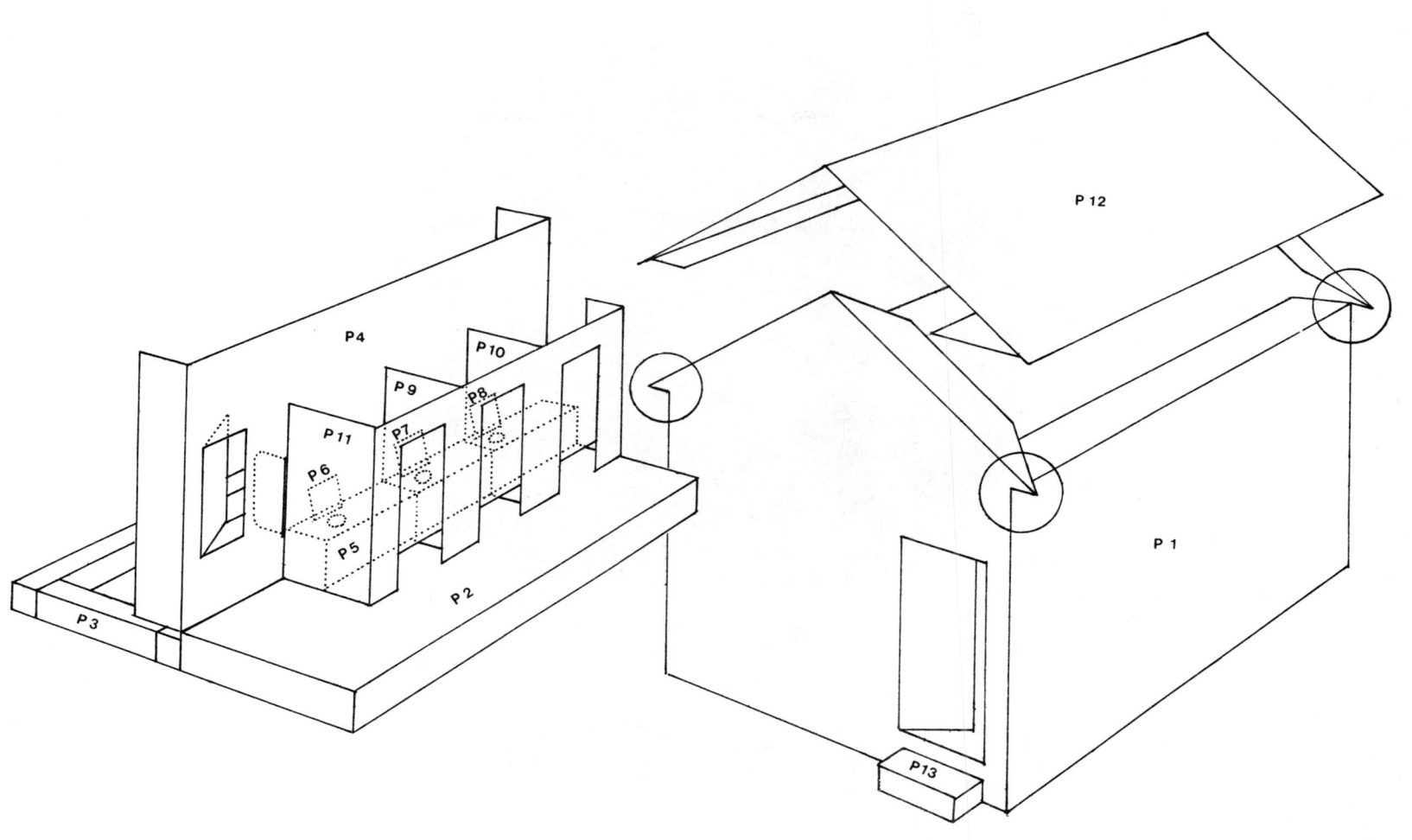

WASHHOUSE

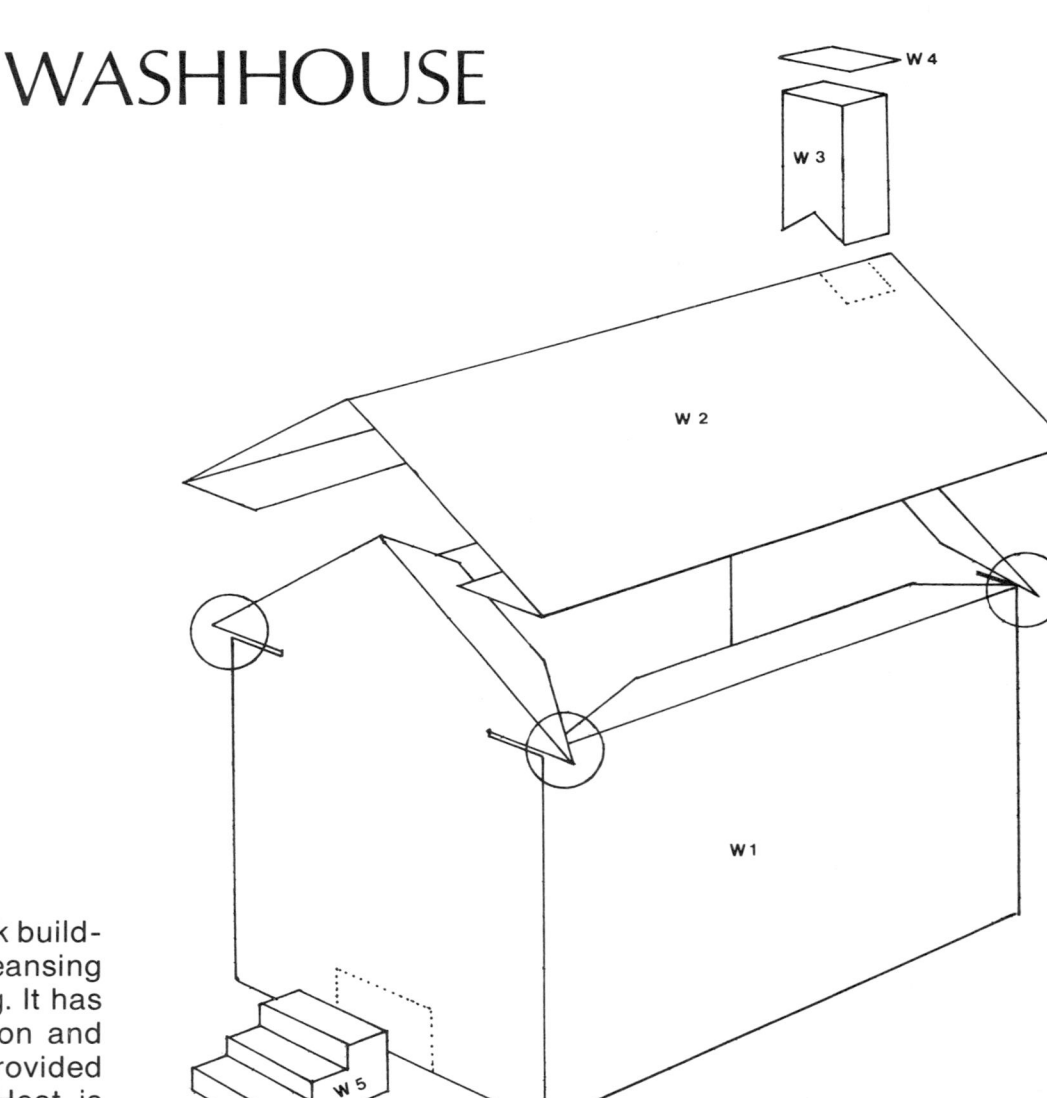

The washhouse is a small brick building used by the ministry for cleansing clothes and for personal bathing. It has two windows for cross ventilation and one door facing south which provided sufficient sun to dry clothes. Heat is provided by a Shaker plate stove.